Handsprings

Poems & Paintings by Douglas Florian

Greenwillow Books
An Imprint of HarperCollinsPublishers

Watercolor paints and colored pencils were used for the full-color art.
The text type is Schneidler.

Library of Congress Cataloging-in-Publication Data

Florian, Douglas.
Handsprings : poems & paintings / by Douglas Florian.
p. cm.
"Greenwillow Books."
ISBN-10: 0-06-009280-7 (trade) ISBN-13: 978-0-06-009280-1 (trade)
ISBN-10: 0-06-009281-5 (lib. bdg.) ISBN-13: 978-0-06-009281-8 (lib. bdg.)
1. Spring—Juvenile poetry. 2. Children's poetry, American. I. Title.
PS3556.L589H36 2005 811'.54—dc22 2005004567

First Edition 10 9 8 7 6 5 4 3 2 1

 Greenwillow Books

ON BLESSED MEMORY OF
BELORIA ABECASSIS LALLOUZ

Contents

WHEN WINTER

When winter winds wind down and end . . .
Then spring is coming round the bend.

When winter ice begins to thaw . . .
Then spring is knocking at the door.

When winter snow is nowhere found . . .
Then spring, you know, has come to town.

Good-bye, winter

Good-bye coat
And good-bye sweater.
Good-bye freezing windy weather.
Good-bye ice
And good-bye snow.
Good-bye winter.
Spring, hello!

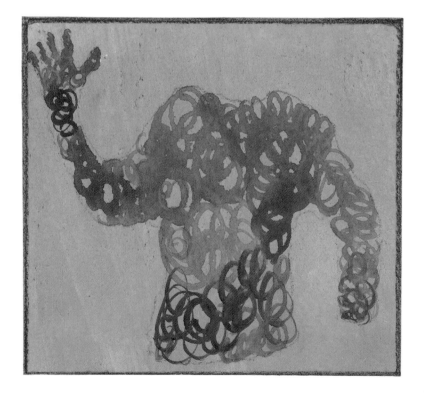

WINTER AND SPRING

Winter's cold and dark and sneezy.
Spring is cool and bright and breezy.
Winter's frigid fingers freezing.
Spring is plentiful and pleasing.
Winter's low in centigrade.
Spring beats winter in the shade!

GROWING

The days are growing l o n g e r.
The sun is growing **stronger**.
The weather's growing milder.
The weeds are growing wilder.
The plants are growing bloomy.

My grin is growing roomy.

HANDSPRINGS

Spring is great
For growing grass.
Spring has zing
And spring has sass.
Spring is super.
Spring is spry.
Spring is when
Things start to fly.
Spring is great
For many reasons.
Spring does handsprings
Round the seasons.

SPRING IS WHEN

Spring is when the geese fly back.
Spring is when I go backpack.
Spring is when the seedlings sprout.
Spring is when groundhogs spring out.
Spring is when I leave my room.
Spring is when there's room to bloom.

WHAT I LOVE ABOUT SPRING

Trees are growing
Streams are flowing
Cool spring showers
Blooming flowers
Caterpillars creep
Peepers peep
Playing sports
Wearing shorts
April Fools'
Swimming pools
Going places
Relay races
Days are longer
Sun is stronger
Every morning songbirds sing—
I love nearly everything!

What i hate about spring

Thunderstorms
Insect swarms
Spring-cleaning
Fixing screening
Pollen spores
Mud outdoors
Bumblebees
Skinned knees
Hot and humid days in June—
I hate that spring goes by too soon.

THE FIRST DAY OF SPRING

The ground is brown.
The trees are bare.
I've still not found
A fox or hare.
No flowers bloom.
No song is sung.
Yet we presume
That spring has sprung.

THE MARCH WIND

The March wind growls.
The March wind howls.
The March wind rattles
And skedaddles.
The March wind whips
And whirls and skips.
Through the larches
The March wind marches.

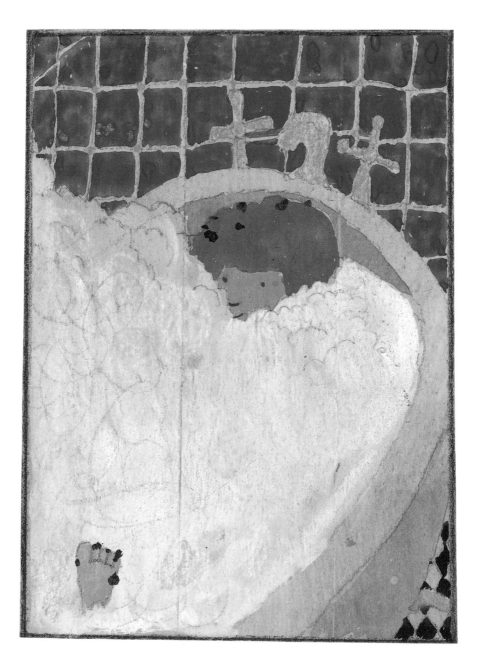

MUD FLOOD

The spring rains came
And made a flood
So now there's mud
    and mud
and mud.
It oozes on my shoes and boots
My pants and shirts and outersuits.
The only cure for springtime muds
Is suds
    and suds
        and suds
           and suds.

Spring sings!
Spring flings
Spring stings
Spring wings
Spring zings
Spring things
Spring brings
Spring shouts
Spring sprouts
Spring zooms
Spring blooms
Spring storms
Spring warms
Spring flows
Spring grows

SPRING

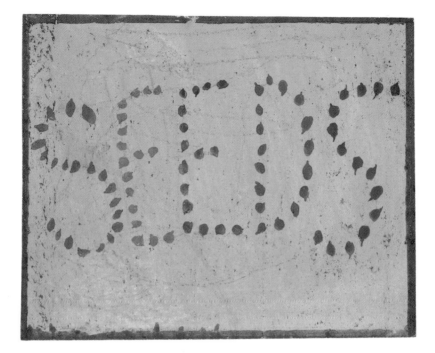

Spring seeds

We tilled the earth,
Took out the weeds,
Then in the soil
Planted seeds:
Pumpkin,
Parsley,
Carrot,
Pea.
Spring succeeds ex-seed-ing-ly.

Spring Training

Our arms are all rusty.
Our pitches are wild.
We're constantly rattled,
And easily riled.
Our bats feel so heavy.
Each hit we misplay.
But soon we'll be ready
For opening day.

Play ball!

The first game of the year.
The first hit.
The first cheer.
The first grand-slam home-run ball
Hit so hard it lands in fall.

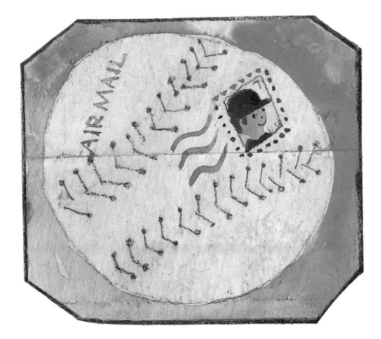

Rain song

I love the gentle *sound* of rain
Pinging on my windowpane.
I love the *sight* of rain that pours
Into puddles out-of-doors.
I love the *feel* of rain that drips
Down my nose and on my lips.

Rain reign

Pop out to play.

The mushrooms all

And rains all day

Each time it rains

Fast indoors.

We hurry, scurry

Each time it pours

Each time it rains

Ten things to do when it rains

Play Ping-Pong.
Sing along.
Read a book.
Learn to cook.
Go exploring
In a drawing.
Write a play.
Talk all day.
Surf the net.
Build a jet.
Or go outside and get wet.

I LOVE LEAVES

I love leaves,
And I love flowers.
I love daydreaming for hours.

I love Aprils.
I love Mays.
I love daydreaming for days.

I love lilies.
I love leeks.
I love daydreaming for weeks.

HEY DAY!

The sky has fell.
The seas are dry.
The fish are swimming in the sky.
The moon is cheese.
There is no school.
And you are such
An April fool!

SPRING-CLEANING

I cleaned my closet.
I cleaned my room.
I cleaned my floor
With mop and broom.
I cleaned the hall.
I cleaned the stairs,
The tabletops, and all the chairs.
I cleaned each musty, dusty thing.
I guess you'd say I cleaned the spring.

SPRING IS

Spring is flowers
        showers
            plowers.
Spring is watching clouds for hours.

Spring is seeding
        weeding
            centipede-ing.
Spring is great for skateboard speeding.

Spring is hiking
        biking
            baseball striking.
Spring's a time to take a liking.

PICKING BERRIES

Picking berries is very fun
Very berry merry fun.
Extra-ordinary fun.
Cherry cheery berry fun.

Spring Berries

Boysenberry
Blackberry
Raspberry
Blue.
Huckleberry
Gooseberry
Teaberry too.
Elderberry
Mulberry
Hawberry
Cran.
Spring brings out
The berry fan.

GREEN SCENE

Cool green
Blue green
Green chartreuse.
Pale green
Yellow green.
Green let loose.
Moss green
Grass green
Grape green,
Lime.
Spring's the bright green
Grown-up time.

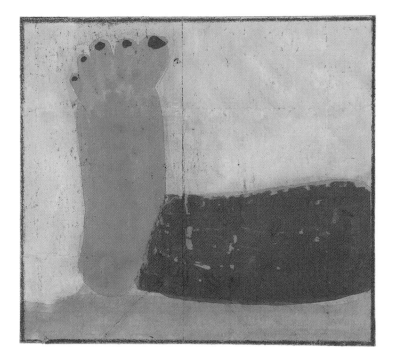

MAY

In May you may run.
In May you may hike.
In May you may skateboard
Or ride on a bike.
In May you may swim
And climb up a tree.
Or fly to the moon—
Well, MAYbe!

SOMETIMES SPRING

Sometimes sun
And sometimes rain—
Spring is one big daisy chain.

Sometimes warm
And sometimes chilly—
Spring is silly daffodilly.

FRESH SPRING

Fresh flowers.
Fresh trees.
Fresh blossoms.
Fresh breeze.
Fresh beetle.
Fresh bee.
Hey Spring, get fresh with me!

Nature walk

On the trail.
Creeping snail.
Bumblebees.
Maple trees.
Maple seeds.
Wild weeds.
White birch bark.
Meadowlark.
Polliwog.
Big bullfrog.
Mountain streams.
Sweet dreams.